HISTORIC PHOTOS OF
LSU FOOTBALL

TEXT AND CAPTIONS BY MARK E. MARTIN AND BARRY C. COWAN

TURNER
PUBLISHING COMPANY

Crowds gather around in 1957 as LSU cheerleaders show off Mike II's new custom-built trailer. Mike would make several appearances on the Tiger field while riding in this trailer.

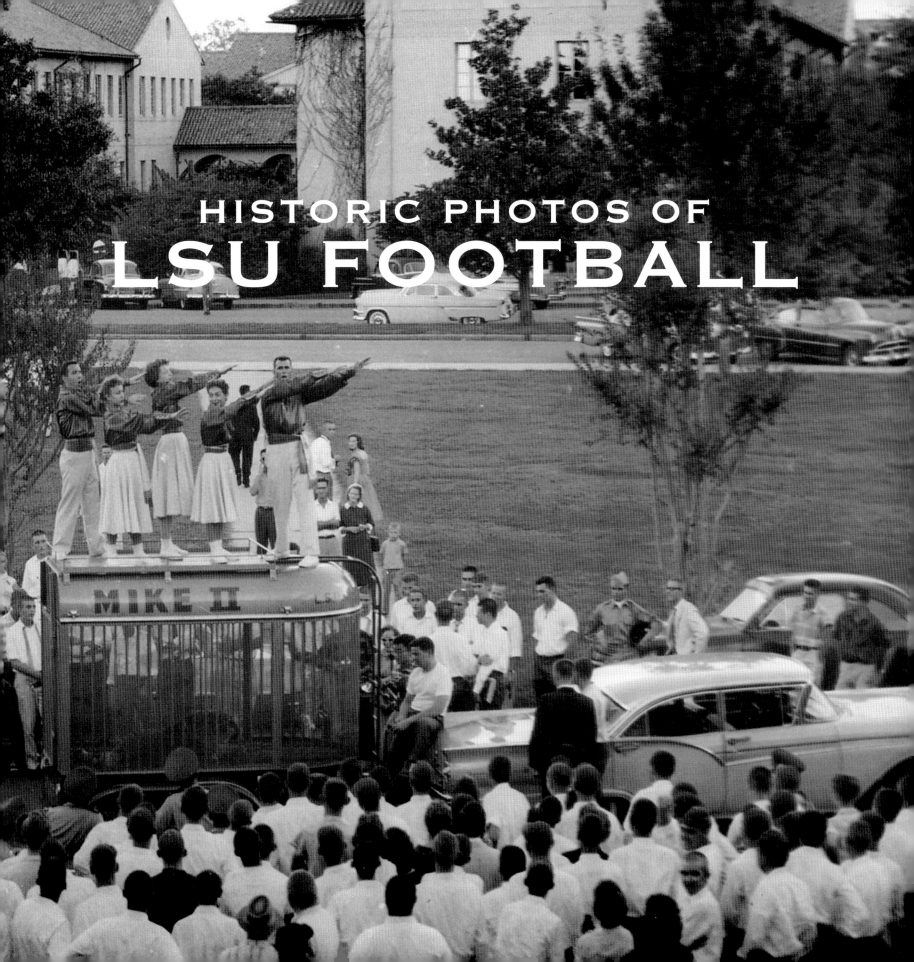

HISTORIC PHOTOS OF
LSU FOOTBALL

Turner Publishing Company
200 4th Avenue North • Suite 950
Nashville, Tennessee 37219
(615) 255-2665

www.turnerpublishing.com

Historic Photos of LSU Football

Library of Congress Control Number: 2009921341

ISBN: 978-1-59652-533-7

Printed in China

09 10 11 12 13 14 15 16—0 9 8 7 6 5 4 3 2 1

CONTENTS

A look at the 1897 team. A pelican motif adorns the sweater of end John T. Westbrook, standing at far-right.

Acknowledgments

This volume, *Historic Photos of LSU Football,* is the result of the cooperation and efforts of many individuals, organizations, and corporations. It is with great thanks that we acknowledge the valuable contribution of the following for their generous support:

Collegiate Images
Louisiana State University Libraries - Special Collections, Hill Memorial Library

We would also like to thank the following individuals for valuable contributions and assistance in making this work possible:

Gabe Harrell and Rachel Bergeron for their digitizing expertise;
Our colleagues for their encouragement;
L.A.B. without whose encouragement none of this would have happened.

———————

With the exception of touching up imperfections that have accrued with the passage of time and cropping where necessary, no changes have been made. The focus and clarity of many images are limited by the technology and the ability of the photographer at the time they were taken.

PREFACE

This project, *Historic Photos of LSU Football*, represents countless hours of review and research. The researchers and writers have reviewed hundreds of photographs. We greatly appreciate the generous assistance of the individuals and organizations listed in the acknowledgments of this work, without whom this project could not have been completed.

The goal in publishing this work is to provide broader access to this set of extraordinary football team photographs that seek to inspire, provide perspective, and entertain. In addition, the book seeks to preserve the past with respect and due reverence.

With the exception of touching up imperfections that have accrued with the passage of time and cropping where necessary, no changes have been made. The focus and clarity of many images are limited by the technology and the ability of the photographer at the time they were taken.

The work is divided into eras. Beginning with some of the earliest known photographs of LSU football, the first section records photographs from the end of the nineteenth century, when the team first held tryouts, to 1908, after the team was officially organized. The second section spans the years from 1909 to 1922, when the team adapted to evolving football rules, suspended games during part of World War I, and organized a cadet band. Section Three moves from the 1920s to the 1930s when the team saw fewer coaches and received instruction under Donahue, Cohen, and Jones. The remaining sections cover the eras under coaches Moore, Tinsley, Dietzel, and McClendon, respectively. In each of these sections, we have made an effort to capture various aspects of LSU football through our selection of photographs, including group shots of the team, photos of coaches, individual players, Mike the Tiger, and LSU rivals as well as famous plays throughout Tiger history.

We encourage readers as they go to a home game in the LSU stadium—also known as "Death Valley"—to reflect on the deep traditions, the long-lasting rivalries, and a few of the outstanding players and coaches who have made LSU football what it is today. It is our hope that in utilizing this work, longtime fans will learn something new and that new fans will gain a perspective on where LSU football has been, so that each can contribute to the team's future.

—Mark E. Martin and Barry C. Cowan

Tyler Lafauci (64), Brad Boyd (89), and Doug Boutte (78) celebrate after winning 20–6 against Auburn in 1973.

THE BEGINNINGS OF LSU FOOTBALL

(1893–1908)

Coach	Years	Season record
Charles E. Coates	1893	0-1
Albert P. Simmonds	1894-95	2-1; 3-0
A.W. Jeardeau	1896-98	6-0; 1-0; 0-1
Edmond A. Chavanne	1898	1-0
John P. Gregg	1899	1-4
Edmond A. Chavanne	1900	2-2
W. S. Borland	1901-3	5-1; 6-1; 4-5
Dan Killian	1904-6	3-4; 3-0; 2-2-2
Edgar R. Wingard	1907-8	7-3; 10-0

1893: LSU's first football game is against Tulane in New Orleans, November 25. Tulane defeats LSU 34–0. Coates never coaches again. LSU players wear gray uniform jerseys with purple trim; LSU's baseball team is the first to wear purple and gold.

1894: Coaches are allowed to play and coach. Coach Simmonds plays in LSU's home game against the University of Mississippi, which LSU loses 26–6 despite Simmonds scoring LSU's only touchdown.

1896: A highlight of the season is LSU protesting Tulane's use of an ineligible player. The Southern Intercollegiate Athletic Association (SIAA) agrees; Tulane forfeits the game.

1897: Only one game is played because of a yellow fever epidemic.

1899: The only victory coach John P. Gregg sees in 1899 comes against Tulane.

1901: LSU protests eligibility of Tulane player Crandall. SIAA rules in LSU's favor, Tulane forfeits the game, and the two teams are banned from playing each other for two years.

1905: Tulane protests five LSU players. These protests are disallowed by Thomas Boyd, LSU's president and SIAA vice-president. College football players suffer 18 deaths and 149 injuries nationally. After President Theodore Roosevelt threatens to outlaw football unless steps are taken to reduce its brutality, the flying wedge at kickoff is banned.

1906: LSU quarterback J. C. Muller throws LSU's first forward pass to B. B. Handy. Bleachers seating 80 fans are constructed at the LSU athletic field. Before this, spectators stood around the sidelines and end zones.

1907: On Christmas Day, LSU and the University of Havana (Cuba) play the first football game outside the U.S. in Havana; LSU wins 56–0.

1908: LSU has one of the heaviest teams in the U.S. with player weight averaging 168 pounds. That year, LSU scored 442 points to their opponents' 11. Tulane again accuses LSU of having ringers but only Mike Lally is ruled ineligible. Coach Wingard resigns at the end of the season and is banned from any connections with an SIAA team.

Charles Coates, LSU's first football coach, was a newly hired chemistry professor from Johns Hopkins who brought football with him when he arrived in 1893.

These cadets showed up for practice in the fall of 1894, but not all were chosen to play. William C. Smedes (holding ball marked LSU) became center, and Samuel Marmaduke Dinwiddie Clark (standing behind Smedes with arms folded) played end and was team captain.

The 1894 team, shown outside the Pentagon Barracks, had a 2-1 record. Coach Albert Simmonds, who played the end position on the 1893 Yale team, is in the front row, fourth from left.

The 1895 team went undefeated with a 3-0 record. Coach Albert Simmonds is wearing the Yale sweater.

The athletic field on the downtown campus was located south of the Pentagon Barracks along the Mississippi River.

The 1897 team played only a two-game season because of a yellow fever epidemic. Coach Allen Jeardeau is at top-row center wearing a suit.

Edmond A. Chavanne played from 1896 to 1899 and was coach and captain of the 1898 and 1900 teams.

Center Leopold Kaffie, seen here in his cadet sergeant's uniform, played in the 1897 and 1898 seasons.

The 1899 Tigers proudly noted on the football that they routed Tulane 38–0, their only win of the season. At top row, wearing cap and bow tie is coach John P. Gregg; to his right is center Edmond A. Chavanne, who would coach again the following year.

The 1900 team had a 2-2 season. Playing Millsaps College twice, the Tigers won 70–0 in Baton Rouge and lost 6–5 in their second meeting in Jackson, Mississippi.

Pictured is the freshman team of 1900. Equivalent to the later junior varsity squads, freshmen were not allowed to play on the varsity team until they became sophomores.

The 1901 football team had a 5-1 record, losing only to Auburn. At left in bowler hat is coach W. S. Borland.

The Tigers defeated Auburn 5–0 in the 1902 game, shown here on LSU's athletic field. Garig Hall is in the background.

The Tigers hover over the Auburn goal line during the 1902 game. The goal posts were homemade, and there seems to have been no crowd control.

The 1902 team finished with a 6-1 record. At center holding the ball is team captain Henry S. Landry. Team members sport an array of protective padding, and two of them have nose guards hanging around their necks.

The 1902 team advertises their victories over Auburn (A.P.I. on football) and the University of Texas at San Antonio by the identical scores 5–0. Coach W. S. Borland is standing at far-right.

The 1905 team went 3-0 defeating Louisiana Polytechnic Institute, Tulane, and Mississippi State. Standing at left is coach Dan Killian.

The Tigers played the first American football game on foreign soil against the University of Havana, defeating them 56–0 on Christmas Day, 1907.

The Tigers were a smaller but faster team than the Havana team. It was reported that the largest men in Cuba were recruited to play for the University of Havana, and that they were fortified with wine dispensed on the sideline.

LSU's first football superstar, 1908: George Ellwood "Doc" Fenton was quarterback from 1907 to 1909. He was known for his speed, toughness, and agility, and could punt, pass, and catch.

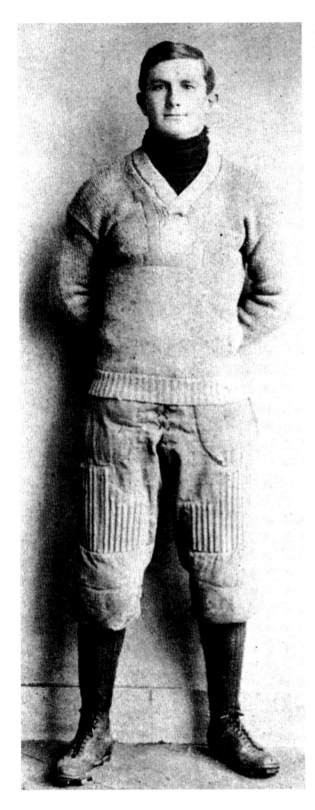

Marshall H. "Cap" Gandy played tackle from 1906 to 1908. A punishing tackler, he was thrown out of a few games for being excessively rough.

The legendary 1908 team had a 10-0 record. At top-row left, wearing a suit, is controversial coach Edgar Wingard and, at center-row left, mascot David Reymond may be seen. Quarterback George E. "Doc" Fenton is in the center row, third from right.

THE EVOLUTION OF A TEAM

(1909–1922)

Coach	Years	Season record
Joe Pritchard	1909	6-2
John W. Mayhew	1909-10	—; 1-5
James K. "Pat" Dwyer	1911-13	6-3; 4-3; 6-1-2
E. T. McDonnell	1914-16	4-4-1; 6-2; 4-1
Irving Pray	1916	2-0
Dana X. Bible	1916	1-0-2
Wayne Sutton	1917	3-5
No football—World War I	1918	—
Irving Pray	1919	6-2
Branch Bocock	1920-21	5-3-1; 6-1-1
Irving Pray	1922	3-7

1909:   Pritchard, a clergyman, resigns after five games to become a missionary in Africa.

1911:   LSU plays Tulane for the first time since 1905, with a 6–0 LSU victory.

1912:   Rules changes make a touchdown score 6 points instead of 5, and the field is shortened from 110 yards to 100 yards with ten-yard end zones.

1913:   Lawrence Dupont scores 15 touchdowns, the most ever by a Tiger in regular season play. LSU players wear numbers for the first time in a game against Tulane.

1914:   The Tigers suffer their worst defeat ever, 63–9 against Texas A&M.

1916:   Three coaches serve at LSU: E. T. McDonnell resigns after five games; Pray, a student at the Audubon Sugar

School, resigns after three games to continue working with sugar chemistry in Cuba; and Dana X. Bible is hired to finish the last three games of the season.

1917:   Because of World War I, many schools don't play during the season. Freshmen are allowed to play on varsity teams for the first time because of the shortage of men. LSU plays at the new State Field located near the Indian mound and arsenal building on what is today the State Capitol grounds.

1918:   No football is played because of World War I.

1919:   Irving Pray returns to coach but resigns at the end of the season and returns to Cuba to concentrate on sugar chemistry.

1920-21:   Branch Bocock serves as coach. He is fired after losing to Tulane two years in a row.

1922:   LSU plays Rutgers for the first time. During the difficult game, Rutgers is penalized 160 yards, and six Tigers are injured. Three days later LSU is defeated by Alabama 47–3. LSU goes on to defeat Tulane 25–14 before 10,000 fans, the largest LSU home crowd ever.

The 1911 team is gathered under the homemade goalposts of LSU's athletic field. Mattresses are attached to the uprights for padding. Coach James K. Dwyer is seen at right.

The 1912 team uses a five-man blocking dummy during practice. They ended the season with a 4-3 record.

Tulane's goat inspects a papier-mâché tiger before the 1912 game held in New Orleans. The Tigers won 21–3.

Tom Dutton had no high school playing experience before coming to LSU in 1911, but at 6 feet 3 inches and 220 pounds, he grew to become a feared tackle.

The 1915 team. Standing at far-left is coach E. T. McDonnell. The condition of the team's uniforms indicates the photograph was taken after a game or practice.

Shown here is the 24-member LSU Cadet Band. This photograph from around 1910 was taken in front of Alumni Memorial Hall.

The 1912 LSU Cadet Band poses in front of the Colony, a dormitory at the downtown campus.

The cadet band stands in formation in this 1916 photograph. LSU supplied the instruments, but a cadet could use his own if he preferred.

In a carnival-like atmosphere, the cadet band is shown in this undated photograph eating boxed lunches.

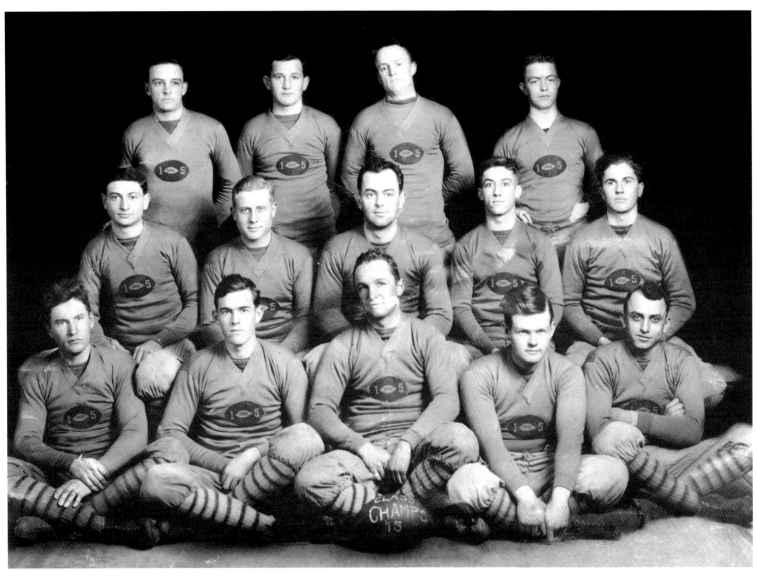

A more formal shot was taken of some of the players from the 1915 team. With a 6-2 record and victories over teams from Louisiana, Mississippi, and Arkansas, they considered themselves champions of three states.

Quarterback Lee Himes was 5 feet 7 inches and weighed 145 pounds when this 1916 photograph was taken.

Six-foot, 167-pound Arthur "Mickey" O'Quinn played
end from 1914 to 1917.

Keith E. "Sweet Papa" Jones played center and guard for the Tigers from 1915 to 1917.

This mock funeral took place after Tulane's loss to LSU in 1922. The headstone reads, "Here Lies Tulane's Goat Beneath this Mount of Green By The Ferocious Tiger Smote To the Dirge 25–14."

These LSU cadets are celebrating the Tigers' victory over Tulane in 1922. The Tigers recorded a 3-7 season, so celebrations such as this were rare that year.

THE DONAHUE, COHEN, AND JONES DECADE

(1923–1934)

Coach	Years	Season record
Mike Donahue	1923-27	3-5-1; 5-4; 5-3-1; 6-3; 4-4-1
Russ Cohen	1928-31	6-2-1; 6-3; 6-4; 5-4
Lawrence "Biff" Jones	1932-34	6-3-1; 7-0-3; 7-2-2

1923:   LSU becomes a member of the Southern Intercollegiate Conference (SIC).

1924:   The Tulane game, Thanksgiving Day, is the first game played in LSU's newly constructed Tiger Stadium on the new campus before the largest football game crowd in Louisiana history; Tulane wins 13–0. This is the first Tiger game broadcast by radio.

1925:   LSU moves to its new campus and suffers its worst home defeat to date against Alabama, 42–0.

1927:   LSU plays Alabama to a scoreless tie, the first time Alabama had not scored in 31 games.

1930:   Governor Huey Long takes an active interest in all things related to LSU football. LSU defeats Arkansas for the first time since 1926 and is then routed by Alabama, 33–0.

1931:   LSU plays its first night game on October 3. Huey Long invites injured players to live at the governor's mansion while they recuperate. Tiger Stadium is expanded to accommodate 20,500 fans.

1932:   Athletic scholarships begin. LSU defeats Tulane for the first time since 1926. Huey Long leads the LSU band through downtown Houston before the Rice game.

1933:   Southeastern Conference (SEC) begins.

1934:   LSU offers $10,000 to Southern Methodist University (SMU) to play in Baton Rouge. Ticket sales are slow with Barnum and Bailey Circus coming to town the same night as the game. Long finds an obscure animal dipping law and threatens to enforce it if Barnum and Bailey doesn't cancel its performance. The circus cancels and game ticket sales surge; LSU pays SMU and makes a profit; the game ends in a tie.

1934:   Before the game with Vanderbilt, Long asks the Illinois Central Railroad to reduce round trip fare to Nashville from $19 to $6. The railroad refuses. Long threatens to raise their taxes from $100,000 to $4 million per year. The railroad relents. Five-thousand LSU fans take the train to Nashville, where Huey leads the crowd on a march; the Tigers win 29–0. Castro Carazo, orchestra leader at the Roosevelt Hotel, New Orleans, is hired by Long to lead the LSU band. Carazo and Long write "Every Man a King" and "Touchdown for LSU."

On Thanksgiving Day 1924, a crowd estimated at 18,000 saw LSU play Tulane in its first game at Tiger Stadium.

These cadets are loading a papier-mâché tiger onto a train leaving for an away game in 1923. The papier-mâché tigers were short-lived, especially if the opposing teams were able to confiscate them.

Jess Tinsley from Haynesville, Louisiana, played tackle from 1926 to 1928 and was named to the All-Southern team in 1928.

Russ Cohen was head coach from 1928 to 1931 and had a 23-13-1 record. An assistant coach at Alabama before coming to LSU, he was a member of Phi Beta Kappa.

This scene of Tiger Stadium was photographed around 1932, the same year that the stadium dormitories were completed. Lights were added a year earlier in 1931, making Tiger Stadium one of the first stadiums in the South to have them.

Bewildered drum major Lew Williams looks on as Huey Long leads the LSU band through downtown Houston prior to the 1932 game with Rice University.

Huey Long bends the referee's ear in Tiger Stadium (ca. 1932). Long sometimes sat with the team and would walk onto the field to dispute a call.

Baton Rouge's Billy Lobdell (with ball) goes around the Rice defense in 1932. Lobdell was the Tigers' quarterback in 1932 and 1933.

The 1908 team and wives held a 25th anniversary reunion and a joint meeting with the Alumni Council on Homecoming Day, October 28, 1933. The former players were honored at the annual L Club banquet.

The 1933 Tiger coaching staff poses for the camera. Standing from left to right are Frank Wandle, Bernie Moore, Joel Hunt, Bert Ingwerson, Lawrence "Biff" Jones, "Spike" Nelson, and Ben Enis.

Center John Kent (left) and "Baby" Jack Torrance were described as "two huskies in the Bengal line." Torrance played guard, tackle, and center and held an Olympic record in the shot put.

Tackle Justin "Iron Man" Rukas makes a hole in the Tennessee defense for Jesse Fatheree (with ball) in 1933. The Tigers defeated the Vols 7–0.

Huey Long enjoys the company of Tiger cheerleaders on the sidelines (ca. 1934).

"Miracle" Abe Mickal played halfback from 1933 to 1935 and was called "a versatile triple-threat performer" who also passed and kicked.

Abe Mickal was not only LSU's star halfback but was also student government president. Huey Long made him a senator in 1934, but Biff Jones objected. Mickal was never sworn in.

Halfback Jesse Fatheree played from 1933 to 1935. He won the Percy E. Roberts Most Valuable Player Award in 1935 for his role in helping the Tigers win their first SEC championship.

THE BERNIE MOORE ERA

(1935–1947)

Coach	Years	Season record
Bernie Moore	1935	9-2, SEC Champions
	1936	9-1-1, SEC Champions
	1937	9-2
	1938	6-4
	1939	4-5
	1940	6-4
	1941	4-4-2
	1942	7-3
	1943	6-3
	1944	2-5-1
	1945	7-2
	1946	9-1-1
	1947	5-3-1

1935: LSU loses season opener to Rice, followed by a 23-game regular season winning streak that ended with a loss against Vanderbilt. Gaynell Tinsley is LSU's first All-American. Huey Long is shot September 8; he dies two days later. LSU loses the Sugar Bowl to Texas Christian (3–2).

1936: Tigers lead the nation in scoring with 281 points. The highest score in Tiger history comes against Southwestern Louisiana Institute, 93–0. The first live LSU mascot, named Mike after athletic trainer Mike Chambers, arrives. Tiger Stadium is expanded. LSU loses second Sugar Bowl to Santa Clara (21–14).

1937:   LSU loses third Sugar Bowl to Santa Clara (6–0), the first time the Tigers have been held scoreless in 50 games.

1938:   Tulane defeats LSU in Tiger Stadium (14–0), resulting in a postgame riot involving an estimated 15,000 people. Afterward, both student bodies declare the playing field off-limits. The "Rag,"a purple and blue flag with the seal of Louisiana in the center, was created to be awarded to the winning school at the post-game banquet.

1939:   Ken Kavanaugh sets records for most consecutive touchdowns and most points scored; he is second LSU All-American and runner-up for the Heisman. The Tigers travel by air for the first time.

1941:   First use of the screen pass by LSU halfback Steve "Moving Van" Van Buren.

1942:   Tailback Alvin Dark is the top scorer in the nation.

1943:   Because of World War II, only four SEC teams play complete schedules. LSU's Steve Van Buren is leading scorer with 98 points, including 16 touchdowns, a record that stands until 1977. LSU wins the Orange Bowl against Texas A&M, 19–14.

1944:   LSU has the worst regular season since 1910.

1945:   LSU's first-ever defeat of Georgia Tech, 9–7, takes place in Atlanta.

1946:   LSU defeats Alabama for the first time in 37 years. The Tigers play Arkansas to a scoreless tie in the Cotton Bowl, also known as the "Ice Bowl." LSU had the most first downs (15 to 1) and most total yardage (271 to 54).

1947:   Bernie Moore, LSU's only coach to win championships in track and football, leaves to become commissioner of the SEC.

End Gaynell "Gus" Tinsley became LSU's first All-American in 1935. He was the Tigers' leading scorer in 1936 with 48 points.

Marvin "Moose" Stewart, center from 1934 to 1936, played the most minutes in 1935 and was an All-American honorable mention.

Bernie Moore was LSU's national championship–winning track coach before becoming football coach in 1935. As head football coach, he boasted an 83-39-6 record and 2 SEC championships.

Facing one another with smiles are Bernie Moore, coach from 1935 to 1947, and Charles Coates, LSU's first football coach in the single-game season of 1893.

From 1934 to 1940, Castro Carazo was leader of the LSU Cadet Band. He is seen here with a drum major and two of the Dancing Tigerettes.

By 1935, Castro Carazo had increased the size of the LSU Cadet Band from about 85 to nearly 250 members.

When Mike the Tiger arrived on October 21, 1936, from the Little Rock Zoo, he was housed at the small City Park Zoo in Baton Rouge.

Upon Mike the Tiger's arrival in 1936, students canceled classes and freshmen blocked professors and anyone carrying books from entering campus.

Tiger Stadium's north end zone was enclosed in 1936, adding additional dormitory rooms and bringing the total number of seats to 46,000.

The LSU Cadet Band salutes Governor Richard Leche for his part in securing federal funds to build the newly completed seating and dormitories in the north end zone. The LSU-Tulane matchup on November 28, 1936, was the first game played in the expanded stadium.

Fullback J. T. "Rock" Reed (at left with ball) outruns the TCU defense in the 1936 Sugar Bowl. The Horned Frogs beat the Tigers 3–2 in this defensive battle.

Halfback Charles "Pinky" Rohm returned 35 punts for 539 yards, including 3 for touchdowns, and was LSU's leading scorer with 54 points in 1937.

Cadet sponsors and Governor Richard Leche (at right) celebrate Mike's second birthday in 1937.

Trainer Mike Chambers (facing camera) sits on the sidelines in 1937. Because Chambers was instrumental in securing LSU's first live tiger mascot, the student body voted to name the tiger Mike.

In 1939, end Ken Kavanaugh became an All-American and led the nation with 30 receptions for 467 yards and 8 touchdowns. Kavanaugh caught 17 touchdown passes from 1937 to 1939.

In 1938, halfback Charles Anastasio (46 with ball) gets a block through the Auburn defense. Anastasio was LSU's leading rusher in 1939.

Mike's new home on campus was completed in 1937. It would change very little until the 1980s.

Enclosing the north end zone of Tiger Stadium added 243 dormitory rooms.

The new north end zone stands, giving a total of 46,000 seats, is shown in this 1938 view.

Leo Bird, the Tigers' leading passer from 1939 to 1941, boots a long punt against Tulane in the 1940 matchup.

The first Homecoming parade was held in Tiger Stadium in 1941. Mike I, first in a long line of tiger mascots, brought up the rear of the parade in his cage.

The Tennessee Volunteers met the Tigers at Homecoming in 1941. This float did not forecast the outcome: the Vols won 13–6.

A float in the 1941 Homecoming parade in Tiger Stadium.

Halfback Alvin Dark played only in 1942 before going off to war, but he became the Tigers' leading rusher (60 attempts for 433 yards) and leading passer with 106 attempts, 40 completions for 556 yards, and 5 touchdowns.

Steve "Moving Van" Van Buren (17) goes around the Georgia Tech defense in 1943. Van Buren led the Tigers that year with 98 points and 847 yards rushing.

Y. A. (Yelberton Abraham) Tittle played quarterback and halfback from 1944 to 1947. In 1946, he fired an 80-yard touchdown pass to Dan Sandifer, one of the longest in Tiger history.

"Beat 'Bama for Bernie" was the cry across campus—and LSU did just that in 1946 by a score of 31–21. It was the first game the two teams had played since 1930.

Called the "Ice Bowl" because of sleet, snow, and freezing temperatures, the 1947 Cotton Bowl ended in a scoreless tie between LSU and Arkansas.

THE TINSLEY YEARS

(1948–1954)

Coach	Years	Season record
Gaynell Tinsley	1948	3-7
	1949	8-3
	1950	4-5-2
	1951	7-3-1
	1952	3-7
	1953	5-3-3
	1954	5-6

1948: Most of the talent under Bernie Moore is gone. Opponents score a record 271 points against the Tigers, who suffer their worst defeat ever against Tulane (46–0). The only bright spot of the season is a conference win against Alabama, 26–6.

1949: The Tigers defeat nearly every team that beat them in 1948. LSU defeats Tulane 21–0 before a record crowd of 79,292. They are routed by Oklahoma in the Sugar Bowl (35–0).

1950: Before the Tulane game in New Orleans, Mike the Tiger is kidnapped by Tulane students and held in Tulane's stadium; he is released to LSU caretakers just before game time with his cage repainted blue and green and festooned with blue and green streamers.

1951: Center George "the Terrible" Tarasovic is named All-American, the first since Kavanaugh in 1939.

1952: For the first time since 1894, the Tigers fail to win a home game. Tinsley introduces a letter-number system for players' uniforms. Ends, guards, and tackles wore E, G, and T (respectively) followed by a number from zero to nine, with the right side of the line wearing even numbers, the left side odd. Centers, quarterbacks, left halfbacks, right halfbacks, and fullbacks wore C, Q, L, R, and F and a zero-to-nine numeral.

1953:   Quarterback Al Doggett completes 68 passes for 822 yards. Tulane is defeated, partially because they begin deemphasizing football, so the annual game slowly loses importance. Tiger Stadium is expanded again for a total of 67,500 seats. The existing stadium is rarely sold out, and the 22,000 new seats cause a problem for Tinsley: How would he be able to fill them?

1954:   LSU loses the first four games, and attendance drops sharply in the newly expanded Tiger Stadium. Tackle Sid Fournet takes All-American. Tinsley is fired at the end of the season with a record of 35-34-6; he didn't win enough games and was thought to have been a weak disciplinarian.

Gaynell "Gus" Tinsley coached the Tigers from 1948 through 1954. Tinsley was believed to have been a lax disciplinarian, and his 35-34-6 record was too uneven for the LSU Board of Supervisors.

On December 1, 1951, the Louisiana State Police studied game day traffic at Tiger Stadium for the Tulane game. In this aerial, Mike the Tiger's cage can be seen between the stadium and the running track.

With 45 points, halfback Kenny Konz was the Tigers' scoring leader in 1950. In the same year, he won the Percy E. Roberts Award for Most Valuable Player.

KENNY KONZ

In 1951, center George "the Terrible" Tarasovic became LSU's first All-American since Ken Kavanaugh received the honor in 1939.

Guard Sid Fournet played from 1951 to 1954. As a freshman, Fournet started every game for the offense in 1951 and became an All-American in 1954. Gus Tinsley called him "the greatest all-around lineman I ever saw at LSU."

In 1952 Gus Tinsley decided to use a letter-number system: for example, Q for quarterback, F for fullback, and T for tackle, accompanied by a number from zero to nine. The system only lasted a year.

A Gator brings down Tiger halfback Charlie Oakley (21 with ball) in the 1953 LSU-Florida game that ended in a 21-all tie.

Receiving the "Rag" for LSU for the fourth consecutive year in 1953 are (left to right) morale commissioner Tom Young, Shirley Thomas, and halfback Jerry Marchand.

The year 1954 was a big one for the big men. End Joe Tuminello (84) was the Tigers' leading receiver with 13 catches for 181 yards and 3 touchdowns. Tackle Sid Fournet (74) was named All-American.

THE DIETZEL ERA

(1955–1961)

Coach	Years	Season record
Paul Dietzel	1955	3-5-2
	1956	3-7
	1957	5-5
	1958	11-0; SEC and National Champions
	1959	9-2
	1960	5-4-1
	1961	10-1; SEC Champions

1955:   Paul Dietzel, 30-year-old offensive line coach at West Point, becomes head coach. LSU's first Homecoming win since 1949 is the first victory over Mississippi State in four years.

1956:   Mike the Tiger dies June 29; his pelt is placed on display at the LSU Museum of Natural Science. Mike II arrives September 28 and is greeted the following day with a parade through downtown Baton Rouge.

1957:   Halfback Billy Cannon, center Max Fugler, halfback Johnny Robinson, and quarterback Warren Rabb join the Tigers. Cannon makes long touchdown runs to defeat Alabama, Texas Tech, and Georgia Tech.

1958:   LSU enters season ranked 35th nationally with a smaller, less experienced team than 1957's. Dietzel divides team into three units: "Chinese Bandits" (defensive specialists), "White" (defense and offense), and "Go" (originally Gold, offense only) teams, allowing fresh players to rotate in and out of games. LSU ends season in first place. Tigers end the regular season by handing Tulane its worst defeat since the series began, 62–0. Tigers outscore opponents 282–53.

Mike II dies; Mike III arrives in August. LSU defeats Clemson in the Sugar Bowl, 7–0, LSU's first Sugar Bowl win in four tries.

1959:   Tigers begin season ranked number 1. At the beginning of the fourth quarter of a Halloween night game, Ole Miss is ahead by a score of 3–0. Cannon returns Ole Miss punt from his own 11-yard line, running it back for the touchdown and eluding at least four defenders along the way. The Tigers win 7–3, and Billy Cannon is awarded the Heisman. Tiger mascot suit worn by a student is introduced. LSU loses to Ole Miss in Sugar Bowl (21–0).

1961:   Roy "Moonie" Winston named All-American. Tigers defeat Georgia Tech 10–0 in Tiger Stadium. GT coach Bobby Dodd said of the game, "It was like the Colosseum in Rome and we were the Christians." Tigers place fourth nationally, and Dietzel accepts his "dream job" as head coach for Army. Tigers win the Orange Bowl against Colorado (25–7) in LSU's second Orange Bowl win and third postseason victory.

Paul Dietzel became the Tigers' head coach in early 1955. His smile shows why he was called "Pepsodent Paul."

LSU played Florida for Homecoming in 1956. The cheerleaders of both teams held a rare joint pep rally before the game.

In 1955 Chi Omega won first place among LSU sororities for their Homecoming display. LSU beat Mississippi State 34–7, the Tigers' first Homecoming win since 1949.

Chuck Johns (with ball) leaps over Joe Tuminello (84) in the 1955 Florida game. Johns was LSU's leading receiver that year with 14 catches for 217 yards and 3 touchdowns.

Baton Rouge's Jimmy Taylor was named to the All-America team in 1957.

Fullback Jimmy Taylor led
the Tigers with 1,312 rushing
yards and scored 127 points
in the 1956 and 1957 seasons
combined. He went on to play
professional football for nine
seasons with the Green Bay
Packers and one season with
the New Orleans Saints.

Mike II and the "Rag" make the traditional round at Tiger Stadium before the 1957 LSU-Tulane game.

As fullback and kicker, Tommy Davis played for the Tigers in 1953. Davis was drafted after the 1953 season and served a hitch in the army. He returned in time to help LSU win its first national championship in 1958.

Tommy Davis' kicking helped win two close games for the Tigers in 1958: one over Florida, 10–7, and another over Mississippi State, 7–6.

Halfback Billy Cannon, a Baton Rouge native who played at Istrouma High School, became the Tigers' rushing and scoring leader. He was named an All-American in 1958 and 1959 and won the Heisman Trophy in 1959.

Billy Cannon (20) and Don "Scooter" Purvis study Paul Dietzel's bulletin board, covered with articles on the Clemson Tigers.
Purvis was a halfback on the Go Team and became an assistant coach under Charles McClendon.

Max Fugler was the White Team's center from 1957 to 1959 and won the Most Minutes Played Award in 1958.

Charles "Bo" Strange, son of assistant coach Clarence "Pop" Strange, played tackle from 1958 to 1960. A member of the White Team, he was an academic All-American in 1960.

The 1958 White Team stands on the field with the LSU stadium in the background. Pictured from left to right are Billy Cannon (20), Johnny Robinson (34), J. W. "Red" Brodnax (36), Paul Dietzel, and Warren Rabb (12).

Halfback for the White Team, Johnny Robinson led the Tigers in 1958 and 1959 with 32 receptions for 416 yards and 7 touchdowns.

After Mike II died in May 1958, students raised $1,500 to purchase and transport Mike III, who arrived on campus in late August. He was introduced to the public on October 4, 1958, during the game against Hardin-Simmons.

The Tigers won the 1958 national championship and SEC championship with a perfect 11-0 season, including a Sugar Bowl win over Clemson.

The Ballet Corps, forerunner of today's Golden Girls, performed with the Tiger Band at halftime. Their capes and coolie hats lie in the grass beside them. The Chinese Bandits had become a crowd favorite, and the band played a special tune after the Bandit defense stopped a drive.

Pictured with cheerleaders in 1959 is a new tiger mascot, a student in a tiger suit.

Paul Dietzel and defensive coach Charles McClendon steer LSU to a 26–3 victory over Rice in 1959.

Halloween night, 1959. With ten minutes remaining in the fourth quarter, Billy Cannon returns an Ole Miss punt from the LSU 11-yard line for a touchdown—and immortality. The Tigers won 7–3, handing the Rebels their first loss of the season.

Billy Cannon eluded seven Ole Miss tackles on his 89-yard touchdown run. The run contributed to his winning the Heisman Trophy.

Two Tiger cheerleaders, the one at right sporting a coolie hat, carry the LSU-Tulane "Rag" before the 1959 matchup. The "Rag" was created in 1939 and went to the winner of the annual game.

Roy "Moonie" Winston, guard from 1959 to 1961, played at Baton Rouge's Istrouma High and became an All-American in 1961. Winston started with the Chinese Bandits in 1959 but moved to the White Team for 1960 and 1961.

Recorded around 1960, this aerial view of Tiger Stadium shows a game-day crowd and the south end zone seats, completed in 1953. Rows of cars surround the stadium and line the nearby streets.

Paul Dietzel and his 1961 Tigers recorded a 9-1 season to become the SEC champions. Dietzel, shown here holding oranges, looked forward to their trip to the Orange Bowl, where they defeated Colorado 25–7.

Fred Miller played tackle for the Chinese Bandits in 1960 and 1961, then moved to the White Team in 1962. In the following ten years, Miller continued his football career as a defensive tackle for the NFL.

THE CHARLES MCCLENDON ERA: THE BEGINNING

(1962–1970)

Coach	Years	Season record
Charles McClendon	1962	9-1-1
	1963	7-4
	1964	8-2-1
	1965	8-3
	1966	5-4-1
	1967	7-3-1
	1968	8-3
	1969	9-1
	1970	9-3, SEC champions

1962:   Charles "Cholly Mac" McClendon becomes head coach. "Hey, Fightin' Tigers" becomes LSU's fight song. Tigers defeat University of Texas in the Cotton Bowl, 13–0, LSU's second bowl victory in a row.

1963:   Injuries result in a difficult season, including a stunning home loss to Ole Miss (37–3). The Kennedy assassination almost cancels the season finale versus Tulane, November 23. The Tigers lose the Bluebonnet Bowl to Baylor.

1964:   In an attempt to reduce injuries, McClendon changes from power sweep plays to a loose flanker offense requiring more finesse. Hurricane Hilda causes postponement of Florida game to season finale; Tigers are defeated 20–6. The Tigers' second Sugar Bowl win comes against Syracuse, 13–10.

1965:   LSU defeats Rice 42–14, the most points scored by the Tigers since 1961. The Baton Rouge Chamber of Commerce estimates LSU football brought nearly $2.8 million into the local economy in 1965, equivalent to $19 million in 2008. The Tigers beat previously undefeated Arkansas in the Cotton Bowl (14–7).

1966:   For LSU's season opener, Paul Dietzel returns to Tiger Stadium as coach of the South Carolina Gamecocks; McClendon's Tigers win 28–13. LSU plays no postseason bowl game for the first time since 1960.

1967:   Tigers defeat Florida for the first time since 1963, lose a close game to Tennessee, and route Mississippi State 55–0. LSU is the SEC's only postseason winner. The Tigers defeat Wyoming in the Sugar Bowl, 20–13.

1968:   LSU is routed by Miami (Florida) 30–0, one of the worst losses of McClendon's career, but they defeat Texas A&M. Tigers win the inaugural Peach Bowl against Florida State (30–27).

1969:   This is an excellent season for McClendon, winning first six games in a row. LSU defeats Auburn, their first game in 27 years. The team's only loss is to Ole Miss. At number 10, LSU does not receive a Bowl berth.

1970:   The Tigers lose to Texas A&M for the first time since 1956. They defeat Alabama for the second year in a row. The Tigers defeat Ole Miss 61–17, taking the SEC title. They lose the Orange Bowl to Nebraska.

From 1961 to 1963, end Billy Truax made crucial plays on offense and defense for the Go Team. In 1963, he led the Tigers with 10 receptions for 112 yards and a touchdown. The same year he was named to the All-America team.

Jerry Stovall from West Monroe, Louisiana, was an All-American and finished second in Heisman voting in 1962.

Halfback Jerry Stovall (21) outruns the Texas Christian University defense.

The Tiger cheerleaders pose here in 1962. Cheerleaders were chosen for a one-year term by both the LSU faculty and the Student Government Association's Morale Commission.

On January 1, 1963, Coach Mac is carried off the field after the Tigers defeat the University of Texas Longhorns, 13–0, in the Cotton Bowl.

Mike III, accompanied by the human Mike mascot, makes the pregame lap of Tiger Stadium (ca. 1964). The cheerleaders on Mike's trailer try to make him roar for the crowd. According to legend, the number of times Mike roars before a game is equal to the number of touchdowns the Tigers will score.

Remi Prudhomme played left guard for the Chinese Bandits in 1962 and 1963. In 1964, he and George Rice became the nucleus of the White Team's defense. He became an All-American in 1964.

Tackle George Rice played on the White Team in 1963 and 1964, and was named to the All-America team in 1965. At 6 feet 3 inches and 250 pounds, Rice, like many other Tigers, went on to compete in the NFL.

Baton Rouge's Doug Moreau was LSU's receiving and scoring leader in 1964 and 1965. He was named All-American in 1965.

With four minutes remaining in the game, Doug Moreau (80) kicks the game-winning field goal in the 1965 Sugar Bowl against Syracuse. The Tigers won 13–10 in their second-ever Sugar Bowl victory.

George Rice (78) runs interference for Sam Grezaffi (30) in the 1965 Tulane game.

The Golden Girls wave from this stationary convertible around 1965. Taking up where the Ballet Corps left off, the Golden Girls entertained at halftime in their gold-sequined outfits.

Defensive end John Garlington played from 1965 to 1967 and was named All-American in 1967. Charles McClendon, who coached the Tigers for nearly 15 years, said of Garlington, "He's the finest I've seen since I've been at LSU."

An elated Charlie McClendon celebrates after defeating Arkansas 14–7 in the 1966 Cotton Bowl. In his grasp is Athletic Director James Corbett. Arkansas was the heavy favorite gunning for a national championship and had won 22 consecutive games prior to the Bowl.

William Swor was director of the "Golden Band from Tigerland" from 1964 to 1977. His elaborate formations helped make the Tiger Band a crowd favorite.

Linebacker George Bevan was the Tigers' leading tackler with 89 tackles in 1967 and 72 tackles in 1969. He was named to the All-America team in 1969.

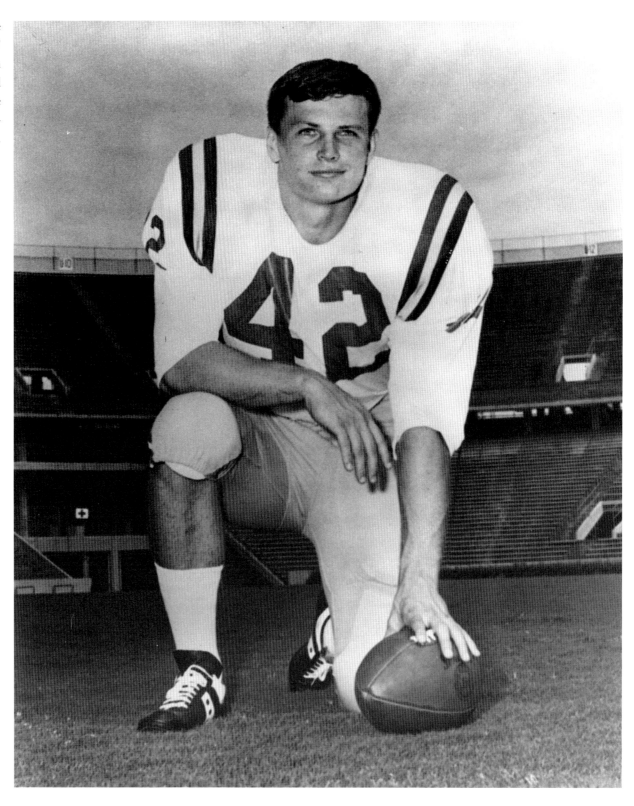

Split end Tommy Morel (80) goes up for a pass during the 1968 game against Texas A&M. The Tigers came from behind to beat the Aggies 13–12.

Fred Haynes (11) is harassed by Aggie Mike Denir (89) in the 1968 game against Texas A&M.

The 1968 Tigers went 8-3 and defeated the Florida State Seminoles 30–27 in the Peach Bowl. As evidenced by this photograph, the team had grown significantly since its first season in 1893.

The Tiger Band had become a crowd favorite with its elaborate formations. This routine, which took shape as a peach tree, was performed during the 1968 Peach Bowl.

Linebacker Mike Anderson, a Tigers fan since his childhood days, played for LSU from 1968 to 1970. He was the Tigers' leading tackler in 1968 with 89 hits. Although he was named All-American in 1970, knee complications prevented him from playing professionally.

LSU celebrated a century in Baton Rouge in 1969 and 1970. This performance featuring a large "100" came during the LSU-Auburn game on October 25, 1969.

The Tigers won the SEC championship in 1970 with a 9-2 regular season record, but lost to Nebraska in the Orange Bowl.

In 1970, Ronnie Estay had the distinction of sacking Joe Theismann of Notre Dame and Archie Manning of Ole Miss, both Heisman contenders for safeties.

Tackle Ronnie Estay (78) wraps up Alabama tight end Glenn Woodruff in 1970. Estay became an All-American in 1971. He later played for the Canadian Football League.

Tommy Casanova, from Crowley, Louisiana, made the All-America team three consecutive years, from 1969 to 1971.

In 1971, *Sports Illustrated* featured safety Tommy Casanova on the cover of its September 13 issue and hailed him as the "best player in the nation."

The LSU Band salutes the University of the Pacific at halftime on October 10, 1970.

The Charles McClendon Era: The Final Years

(1971–1979)

Coach	Years	Season record
Charles McClendon	1971	9-3
	1972	9-2-1
	1973	9-3
	1974	5-5-1
	1975	5-6
	1976	7-3-1
	1977	8-4
	1978	8-4
	1979	7-5

1971: Tigers defeat Notre Dame 28–8. LSU defeats Iowa State in the Sun Bowl, 33–15. McClendon considers a ten-year, $1 million contract offer from Texas A&M but takes a five-year contract with LSU.

1972: LSU is the number one pick. The Tigers win the first seven games, including a one-point victory over Ole Miss in the last two seconds of the game. Alabama is their only regular season loss. LSU loses the Astro-Bluebonnet Bowl to Tennessee, 24–17. Cornerback Mike Williams is the first LSU African-American player from Louisiana.

1973: LSU wins first nine games but loses to Tulane 14–0, the first time since 1948. Alabama defeats Tigers in Tiger Stadium 21–7. LSU loses Orange Bowl to Penn State, 16–9.

1974: Very inconsistent play results in loss of 29 of 49 fumbles.

1975: This is McClendon's only losing season, but the Tigers defeat Tulane in the Superdome.

1976: NCAA forfeits the Mississippi State game to LSU. Tigers hold number one–ranked Nebraska to a 6–6 tie.

Tigers rout Ole Miss 45–0. Mike III dies; August Busch III donates Mike IV to LSU.

1977:   LSU wins three of four of its regular season road games. Charles Alexander, offensive star, sets an SEC record, rushing 1,686 yards in 311 carries. Tigers lost to Indiana (24–21) in front of 78,534 fans. LSU loses the Sun Bowl to Stanford.

1978:   Work is completed on Tiger Stadium west-side expansion of 7,500 seats. Dietzel returns to LSU as athletic director and proposes extending McClendon's contract until the end of the 1979 season, when McClendon would have stepped down as coach. This allows McClendon to serve as president of the American Football Coaches Association. The Tigers beat Indiana 24–17. They lose the Liberty Bowl to Missouri.

1979:   LSU wins first two games but loses to USC before the second-largest crowd in Tiger Stadium history. They defeat Ole Miss but lose to Tulane—their opponent's second victory since 1948. McClendon wins his final game in Tiger Stadium against Mississippi State; his last game is the Tangerine Bowl win against Wake Forest.

During his career as head coach for the Tigers, McClendon had the most wins of any LSU coach, 137-59-7. His teams earned an SEC championship, won 7 of 13 bowl games in 18 seasons, and produced 17 first-team All-Americans and 53 first-team All-SEC players.

In 1972 and 1973, Linebacker Warren Capone was an All-American and LSU's leading tackler with 141 tackles.

On October 2, 1971, Mike the Tiger, two drum majors, and a baton twirler lead the Tiger Band down Victory Hill toward Tiger Stadium. The march took place just before the Rice game.

Bert Jones completed 28 passes for touchdowns from 1970 to 1972. Jones was the Tigers' leading passer in 1971 and 1972.

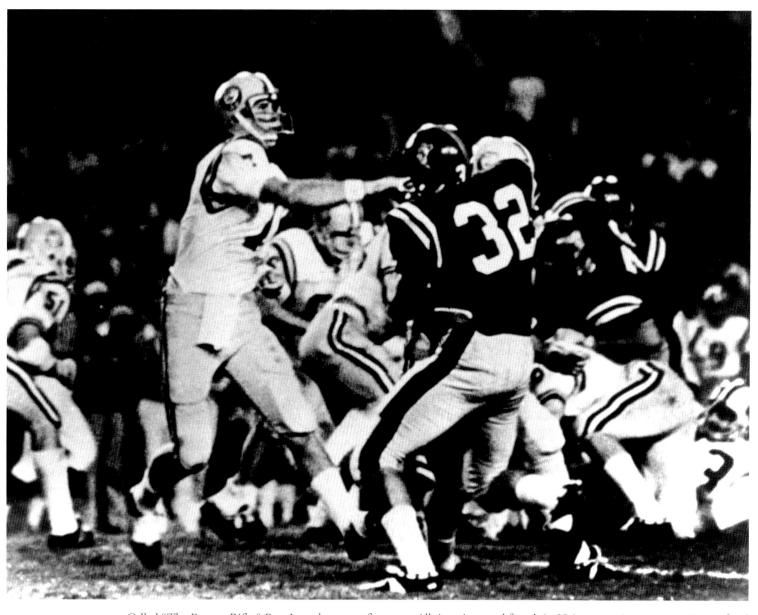

Called "The Ruston Rifle," Bert Jones became a first-team All-American and fourth in Heisman voting in 1972. He ran for 4 touchdowns and passed for 14 more that year.

As seen in this photograph, Bert Jones shows form tailored more for the dropback pass instead of running the option.

On October 14, 1972, Governor Edwin Edwards presents Castro Carazo with a proclamation honoring him for his services as bandleader in the 1930s. Carazo wrote "Touchdown for LSU," "Darling of LSU," and "Every Man a King."

During his time at LSU, Tyler Lafauci became quite accomplished. As guard from 1971 to 1973, Lafauci was an academic All-American, an athletic All-American, and the winner of the Roberts-Eastland MVP Award in 1973.

In the final second of the 1972 LSU–Ole Miss game, Heisman candidate Bert Jones passes to Brad Davis. Davis makes the touchdown with no time left on the clock.

Al Coffey (3) and Gerald Keigley (34) celebrate Davis' touchdown, while Rebel Harry Harrison (30) falls to his knees in shock.

As the crowd goes wild, Ken Addy (45) and Jones (7) join the team's celebration.

All eyes of the audience are on the ball as Rusty Jackson's (8) extra-point kick sails over the goal posts, giving the Tigers a 17–16 win over Ole Miss. Charles McClendon said of the Tiger triumph, "You'd have to call this one victory one of the all-time thrills in Tiger history."

The LSU bench pours onto the field to celebrate the close victory.

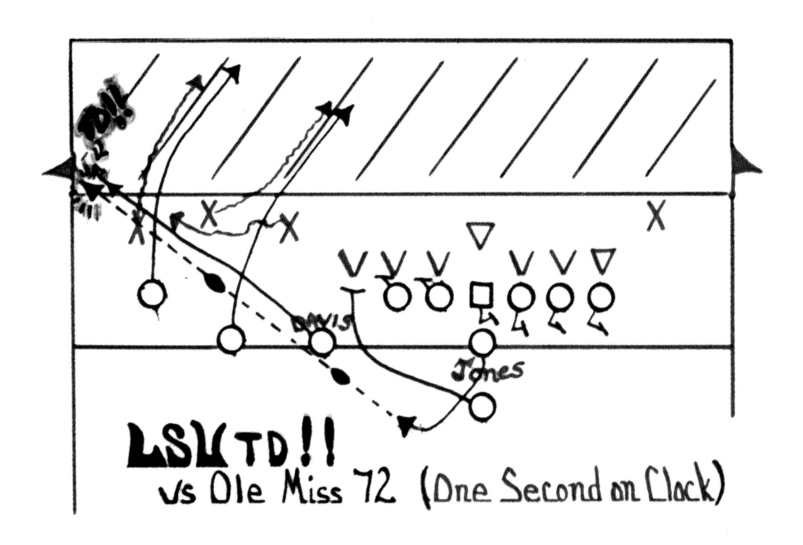

This is a diagram drawing of the play that won the 1972 LSU–Ole Miss game.

In 1971, Lora Hinton received a football scholarship from LSU. Originally from Virginia, he was the first African-American to receive such a scholarship. As fate would have it, Hinton had to sit out the 1972 season due to a knee injury.

Running back Lora Hinton (24) goes through the Ole Miss defense. He was a three-year letterman from 1973 to 1975.

In 1972, Mike Williams of Covington, Louisiana, was the first African-American to play for the Tigers.

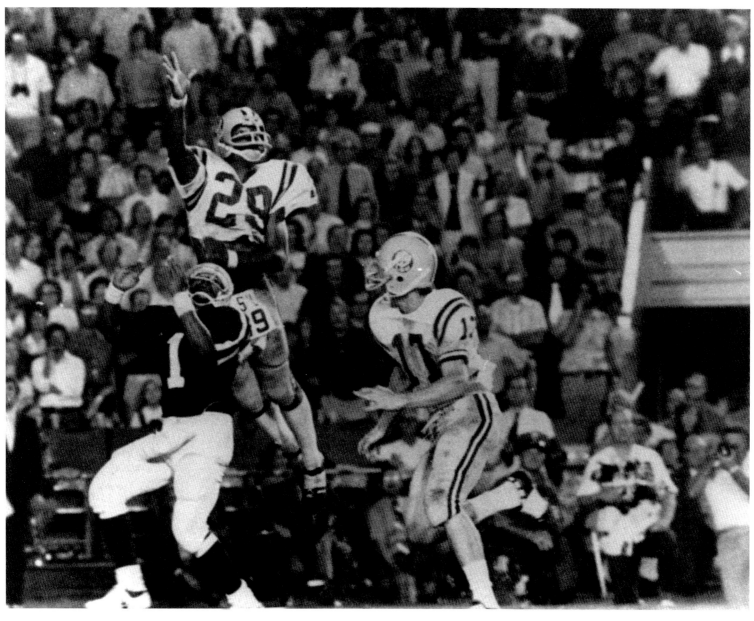

Cornerback Mike Williams (29) goes after the ball in this photograph full of momentum. He was a three-year letterman, from 1972 to 1974.

From 1973 to 1976, tackle A. J. Duhe, from Reserve, Louisiana, was the heart of the Tiger defense.

Tailback Brad Davis (48) gets past the Colorado defense in 1973. The Tigers won 17–6.

"Miracle" Mike Miley, who completed 60 passes for 978 yards and 7 touchdowns in 1973, launches one during that year's Auburn game.

Billy Broussard (9) from Jennings, Louisiana, lofts a pass over the Mississippi State defense in the 1974 meeting. Broussard was the Tigers' leading passer that year.

Brad Davis (carrying ball) is pursued by the Florida defense in the 1974 game. Davis was LSU's leading rusher and scorer that year with 701 yards and 54 points.

Charles Alexander was one of the Tigers' all-time leading rushers with 4,035 yards and 40 touchdowns between 1975 and 1978.

By 1975 several student groups, including the Interfraternity Council, began soliciting donations to improve Mike's living conditions. Many believed his cage was too small and did not provide a healthy habitat.

Pictured here in 1975 is Mike IV's habitat. It would not be enlarged until the early 1980s.

Tallulah, Louisiana, split back Carl Trimble (3) catches a pass during the 1976 Tulane game. Trimble was the Tigers' leading receiver in 1975 and 1976.

Just as they had in 1955, in 1977 Chi Omega won first place among the sororities for their Homecoming display. The 1977 football team, however, wound up sharing dinner with Kentucky, which defeated the Tigers 33–7.

Tailback Hokie Gajan (47) eludes the Ole Miss defense on the way to a 28–21 Tiger victory in 1977.

Running back Charles Alexander was an All-American in 1977 and 1978. During the 1977 season, he set an SEC record when he rushed for 1,686 yards.

Charles Alexander eludes the University of Oregon defense on October 22, 1977, on his way to helping score a 56–17 Tiger victory.

Originally named Jerry when he was born in 1974 at Busch Gardens in Tampa, Mike IV arrived on campus in August 1976, weighing 450 pounds. He reigned until 1990.

Construction of 8,000 additional seats on Tiger Stadium's west upper deck began in 1976.

Around 1978, the Golden Girls perform in Tiger Stadium during halftime. The band accompanies their routine.

Defensive tackle Robert Dugas, playing from 1976 to 1978, became an academic All-American in 1977 and an athletic All-American in 1978.

By 1979, Baton Rouge native quarterback Steve Ensminger (5) was part of a two-pronged offense: Ensminger was the passing quarterback, while David Woodley was the more mobile quarterback who could run the option.

The west upper deck, seen at right, enabled 79,940 fans to experience the action in Tiger Stadium. The new section was ready for the 1978 season opener against Indiana, which the Tigers won 21–17. The band on the field is spelling LSU.

Coach McClendon is carried off the field after defeating Mississippi State 21–3 on November 17, 1979. It was the last game "Cholly Mac" would coach in Tiger Stadium.

Notes on the Images

These notes, listed by page number, attempt to include all aspects known of the images. Each image is identified by the page number, photograph's or drawing's title or description, photographer or artist and collection, archive, and call or box number when applicable. Although every attempt was made to collect all data, in some cases complete data may have been unavailable due to the age and condition of some of the images and records.

II MIKE II'S NEW TRAILER
LSU-Collegiate Images
Folder 1 - Mike II arriving on campus 1958

VI LSU TEAM, 1897
LSU-Collegiate Images
a50000533

X VICTORY OVER AUBURN, 1973
LSU-Collegiate Images
Lafauci, Boyd, etc celebrating

3 PORTRAIT OF CHARLES COATES
LSU-Collegiate Images
Folder 21 - Portrait of Charles Coates

4 FALL TRY-OUTS, 1894
LSU-Collegiate Images
a50000495

5 THE 1894 TEAM OUTSIDE BARRACKS
LSU-Collegiate Images
a50000532

6 COACH SIMMONDS UNDEFEATED TEAM, 1895
LSU-Collegiate Images
a50000514

7 DOWNTOWN CAMPUS ATHLETIC FIELD
LSU-Collegiate Images
a50000313

8 COACH JEARDEAU TEAM, 1897
LSU-Collegiate Images
a50000573

9 EDMOND A. CHAVANNE
LSU-Collegiate Images
a50000243

10 LEOPOLD KAFFIE
LSU-Collegiate Images
a50000230

11 TIGERS GROUP PORTRAIT, 1899
LSU-Collegiate Images
a50000536

12 THE 1900 TEAM
LSU-Collegiate Images
a50000515

13 THE FRESHMAN TEAM OF 1900
LSU-Collegiate Images
a50000516

14 COACH BORLAND'S 1901 TEAM
LSU-Collegiate Images
a50000113

15 DEFEAT OF AUBURN, 1902
LSU-Collegiate Images
a50000109

16 AT THE AUBURN GOAL LINE, HOPING TO SCORE
LSU-Collegiate Images
a50000111

17 TEAM CAPTAIN LANDRY AND 1902 TEAM
LSU-Collegiate Images
a50000114

18 ENJOYING THE VICTORY
LSU-Collegiate Images
a50000475

19 COACH KILLIAN AND 1905 TEAM
LSU-Collegiate Images
a50000115

20 FIRST AMERICAN GAME ON FOREIGN SOIL
LSU-Collegiate Images
1907 team in Havana

21 THE TEAM IN HAVANA
LSU-Collegiate Images
Folder 4 - When Tigers took Cuba

22 GEORGE FENTON, FIRST SUPERSTAR
LSU-Collegiate Images
fentondoc

23 TACKLE MARSHALL GANDY
LSU-Collegiate Images
1908 - MH Gandy, descreened

24 COACH WINGARD AND 1908 TEAM
LSU-Collegiate Images
a50000118

27 COACH DWYER AND 1911 TEAM
LSU-Collegiate Images
1912 - 1911 football team, descreened

160 **TOMMY CASANOVA**
LSU-Collegiate Images
Tommy Casanova

161 **CASANOVA WITH BALL**
LSU-Collegiate Images
TommyCasanova-105

162 **BAND FORMATION 1970**
LSU-Collegiate Images
Folder 25_Heart done by
the band of the University of
Pacific_California_ Oct.10
1970

165 **WARREN CAPONE**
LSU-Collegiate Images
Warren Capone

166 **TIGER BAND ON VICTORY
HILL, 1971**
LSU-Collegiate Images
Folder 33_Drum Major with
tiger_Oct.2 1971

167 **BERT JONES**
LSU-Collegiate Images
Bert Jones

168 **BERT JONES IN ACTION**
LSU-Collegiate Images
jones1

169 **BERT JONES WITH THE
BALL**
LSU-Collegiate Images
Bert Jones 1

170 **SALUTE TO CASTRO
CARAZO**
LSU-Collegiate Images
Salute to Carazo_Oct.14
1972_Edwin Edwards and
Castro Carazo

171 **TYLER LAFAUCI**
LSU-Collegiate Images
Folder 2 - Tyler LaFauci

172 **BERT JONES TO BRAD
DAVIS**
LSU-Collegiate Images
1973 - p 284 - Jones Passes

173 **SURPRISE VICTORY
CELEBRATION**
LSU-Collegiate Images
1973 - p 285 - 34 receives

174 **SURPRISE VICTORY
CELEBRATION NO. 2**
LSU-Collegiate Images
1973 - p 285 - 45, 7 run to
end zone

175 **RUSTY JACKSON'S
EXTRA POINT**
LSU-Collegiate Images 1973-
p 284 - 8 kicks extra point

176 **SURPRISE VICTORY
CELEBRATION NO. 3**
LSU-Collegiate Images
1973 - p 285 - Celebration

177 **DIAGRAM OF GAME-
WINNING PLAY**
LSU-Collegiate Images
1973 - p 285 - Play Diagram

178 **LORA HINTON**
LSU-Collegiate Images
Folder 8 - Lora Hinton

179 **LORA HINTON IN
ACTION**
LSU-Collegiate Images
Folder 8 - Lora Hinton on
field

180 **MIKE WILLIAMS**
LSU-Collegiate Images
Folder 20 - Mike Williams

181 **MIKE WILLIAMS IN
ACTION**
LSU-Collegiate Images
Folder 8 - Mike Williams

182 **A. J. DUHE**
LSU-Collegiate Images
A.J. Duhe

183 **BRAD DAVIS IN ACTION**
LSU-Collegiate Images
1974 - p387 - Brad Davis 1973

184 **MIKE MILEY IN ACTION**
LSU-Collegiate Images
1974 - p393 - Mike Miley

185 **BILLY BROUSSARD IN
ACTION**
LSU-Collegiate Images Miss
State 1974 - Tiger 9 w ball

186 **BRAD DAVIS WITH THE
BALL**
LSU-Collegiate Images
1975 - p281 - 48 Carrying
the Ball

187 **CHARLES ALEXANDER**
LSU-Collegiate Images
alexandercharles

188 **SOLICITATIONS FOR
MIKE**
LSU-Collegiate Images
1976 - p97 - Donations for
Improvements

189 **MIKE IV'S HABITAT**
LSU-Collegiate Images
1976 - p97 - Mike's Habitat

190 **CARL TRIMBLE IN
ACTION**
LSU-Collegiate Images
1977 - p232 - 3 catching ball

191 **SORORITY FIRST-PLACE
HOMECOMING DISPLAY,
1977**
LSU-Collegiate Images
1978 - p175 - Chi Omega
homecoming decorations

192 **HOKIE GAJAN IN
ACTION**
LSU-Collegiate Images
1978 - p177 - 47 carrying ball

193 **CHARLES ALEXANDER
WITH THE BALL**
LSU-Collegiate Images
alexandercharles2

194 **CHARLES ALEXANDER IN
ACTION**
LSU-Collegiate Images
Folder 2 - Charles Alexander

195 **MIKE IV**
LSU-Collegiate Images
Folder 23 - Mike IV

196 **ADDITIONS TO TIGER
STADIUM**
LSU-Collegiate Images
Tiger Stadium construction_
1936

197 **GOLDEN GIRLS
PERFORMANCE**
LSU-Collegiate Images
Golden Girls c.1978

198 **ROBERT DUGAS**
LSU-Collegiate Images
Folder 20 - Robert Dugas

199 **STEVE ENSMINGER IN
ACTION**
LSU-Collegiate Images
ensmingersteve

200 **TIGER STADIUM'S NEW
WEST UPPER DECK**
LSU-Collegiate Images
lsu_tiger stadium

201 **COACH MCCLENDON
CARRIED OFF FIELD**
LSU-Collegiate Images
CharlesMcClendon-103